QUICK GUIDE TO FANTASY SPORTS

QUICK GUIDE TO FANTASY HOCKEY

by Erin Nicks

BrightPoint Press

San Diego, CA

BrightPoint Press

an imprint of ReferencePoint Press, Inc.
Printed in the United States

For more information, contact:
BrightPoint Press
PO Box 27779
San Diego, CA 92198
www.BrightPointPress.com

LIBRARY OF CONGRESS CATALOGING-IN-PUBLICATION DATA

Names: Nicks, Erin, author.
Title: Quick guide to fantasy hockey / by Erin Nicks.
Description: San Diego, CA : ReferencePoint Press, [2021] | Series: Quick guide to fantasy sports | Includes bibliographical references and index. | Audience: Grades 10-12
Identifiers: LCCN 2020002641 (print) | LCCN 2020002642 (eBook) | ISBN 9781678200060 (Hardcover) | ISBN 9781678200077 (eBook)
Subjects: LCSH: Fantasy hockey (Game)--Juvenile literature.
Classification: LCC GV1202.F345 N54 2021 (print) | LCC GV1202.F345 (eBook) | DDC 793.93--dc23
LC record available at https://lccn.loc.gov/2020002641
LC eBook record available at https://lccn.loc.gov/2020002642

CONTENTS

AT A GLANCE 4

INTRODUCTION 6
FIGHTING FOR THE CHAMPIONSHIP

CHAPTER ONE 14
WHAT IS FANTASY HOCKEY?

CHAPTER TWO 24
WHICH LEAGUE TO CHOOSE?

CHAPTER THREE 42
HOW DO OWNERS DRAFT TEAMS?

CHAPTER FOUR 58
HOW DO OWNERS BUILD A WINNING TEAM?

Glossary 74
Source Notes 75
For Further Research 76
Index 78
Image Credits 79
About the Author 80

AT A GLANCE

- Fantasy hockey participants draft teams and earn points based on NHL players' performances.
- Fantasy hockey is a game that can be played by anyone. It can be played online or offline.
- There are many different types of fantasy hockey leagues. Some types include box, head-to-head, rotisserie, and keeper.
- There are also different types of drafts. Some draft types include standard linear, snake, and auction style.
- Strategy is important when preparing for a draft. Think about the categories a league has and where the most points can be gained.
- Always draft the best players available.

- Star forwards are important, but don’t forget about offensive defensemen. They pick up a lot of assists.
- Use your resources. Hockey magazines give player breakdowns before the NHL season begins.
- Don’t forget to read the news from sports reporters. They will have up-to-date information on player injuries and lineup changes, in case you need to shuffle your team.

FIGHTING FOR THE CHAMPIONSHIP

In the National Hockey League (NHL), games can come down to the final moments. The same is true in fantasy hockey. The Colorado Avalanche were playing the San Jose Sharks. Meanwhile, two fantasy owners, Brian and Katie, were fighting it out for the league championship.

Fantasy hockey is a great way to engage with the NHL in a new way.

They were part of a fantasy league with friends from school. As the NHL season progressed, Brian and Katie topped their league in points. So far, Brian's team had scored 220 points that season. He was in the lead by two points. But he didn't have

Goaltenders can be pulled so teams can use an extra forward or defenseman.

any NHLers on his team playing in the last game. Katie only had one skater in the game: San Jose's Brent Burns.

Burns had scored in the first period. Brian and Katie's league gave two points for a goal. This meant they were tied. Katie hoped Burns would score another point. Assists were worth one point. Katie only needed one point to win. In the third period with just over four minutes left, Joe Pavelski looked like he had scored an **empty-net goal**. Katie was sure Burns had also touched the puck. This would have given her the assist point she needed. But the goal did not count. Katie was worried. Would Burns ever get another point? Time was running out. She looked down at her phone. Brian had sent a text. He was already joking about splitting the win. “I get to lift the trophy first,” he wrote.

The score was 4–2. San Jose was going to win the game. But the night was not over for the fantasy players. First place in the fantasy league was decided with 45 seconds left in the third period. Micheal Haley of the Sharks scored an empty-net goal. But were there any assists? The announcer finally took the mic: “Goal scored by Micheal Haley at 19:15, with assists by Barclay Goodrow and Brent Burns!” Katie got her extra point. She had won the league

Just as NHL teams compete for the Stanley Cup, some fantasy leagues compete for trophies.

and the right to keep the league's trophy for the whole year.

GETTING INVOLVED

Fantasy hockey is an exciting game. It can be played anywhere. It helps NHL

Fantasy owners often follow new teams or watch games they might not have otherwise.

fans experience hockey in a new way. Games that may not matter for playoff standings can become must-see television. League players battle each other for points until the last game of the season. It is a great way to have fun with friends on any night of the week.

CHAPTER ONE

WHAT IS FANTASY HOCKEY?

Fantasy hockey follows teams created by fans. Participants are called team owners. They pick NHL players. These players earn points for their team. Points are given for different actions during an NHL game. Players score points for anything from goals to fights. The owner with the

Fantasy hockey uses the statistics earned by NHL players.

most points at the end of the season wins. Some leagues also play during the postseason. Owners stay busy throughout the entire year. They draft new players. They trade players with other owners. They think about rule changes for their fantasy league. Owners also pay attention to hockey news. They watch for new players who might be great. Owners want as many superstars as possible. But they also want lesser-known players who might suddenly score many points. These players are called **sleepers**. "The right sleeper can alter a fantasy hockey season," said Matt Larkin of The Hockey News.[1]

HOW DID FANTASY HOCKEY START?

No one knows when the first official fantasy league began. But one early league started in 1981. Ten people working in the Madison

One of the first fantasy leagues started in the Madison Square Garden press room.

Square Garden press room came up with a game. They held a draft. They picked NHL players for their teams. They would add the goals the players scored. The team with the most goals at the end of the year won. Neil Smith was one of the owners. He was a scout for the New York Islanders. He later became general manager of the New York Rangers. "It was called the OIHL, I made up that name," said Smith. "It was Office Hockey League to represent everyone in the office, but it was also Off-Ice Hockey League. It was fun."[2]

Today's technology makes fantasy hockey easy to play. Fans use the

ONLINE, ANYTIME

An owner can start playing anytime throughout the NHL season. Many leagues allow an owner to play for as long as they like. Some leagues even pick teams for one night. Owners choose players from teams playing that day. The owner with most points at the end of the night wins.

internet to learn updates on any athlete. Stats are updated twenty-four hours a day. Information from sports media helps owners. They can learn about injuries, **healthy scratches**, and starting goaltenders. Before the internet, leagues like the OIHL could only use whatever information they could get. News came into the press box. Owners could learn when goals were scored throughout the NHL.

Sam Rosen was another member of the OIHL. He is the play-by-play announcer for the Rangers. "We had great times. We had our draft set up and dinner was

New York Rangers announcer Sam Rosen was part of the OIHL.

brought in at the press room at Madison Square Garden," said Rosen. "We had a night where the WWF [World Wrestling Federation] had 20,000 people screaming in the building and we'd be in our press room conducting our OIHL draft."[3]

HOW DO YOU PLAY FANTASY HOCKEY?

One of the easiest ways to play is to join an online league. Websites like Sportsnet.ca, CBSSports.com, and ESPN.com run some of the biggest leagues. Owners can play on their own. Many play against other hockey fans. They can invite their friends to join.

PICK ANY PLAYER

Simulated hockey is a type of league. It allows owners to pick players from any time in NHL history. That means a player could draft former stars Wayne Gretzky and Martin Brodeur for their team. Websites use information about these players to figure out how many points they earn.

Leagues are often made of friends or family members.

Each league has different rules. Basic leagues will often use similar point systems. Owners get one point for a goal or an assist. They get two points for a goaltender win. They also get one point for a shootout or overtime loss. They get an extra point for a shutout. Leagues often have owners set a weekly lineup.

Many people play with friends. They may also play with strangers online. Some leagues create their own rules. Others use a website's rules. There are many different types of leagues. There are keeper leagues, rotisserie leagues, and daily leagues. There are even leagues where owners select players from the NHL's history. Some owners follow hockey just a little. Others are hardcore fans. There is a league out there for everyone.

CHAPTER TWO

WHICH LEAGUE TO CHOOSE?

There are many types of leagues. Owners must choose one that is right for them. An owner must decide if they want to play alone or against friends. They need to consider how much time they have. Different leagues need different amounts of work. Box leagues can be done in a few minutes. Owners usually keep the same

There are many different types of leagues. Each kind requires different strategies and levels of commitment.

players all season. A keeper league needs more attention. Players are traded. Rosters are changed. Before beginning, owners must understand how their league works. "Before you even begin to research players,

A high-scoring player like Colorado's Nathan MacKinnon is a valuable asset on a fantasy hockey team.

make sure you understand the rules of your league," says Josh Beneteau of Sportsnet. "Every league is different, and every league counts different stats which will change how you should value certain players."[4]

BOX LEAGUES

Box leagues are one of the easiest ways to play. Players of similar talent are grouped into boxes. The groups usually have four or five players. The **draft manager** organizes the boxes. Websites can also make the groupings. Player positions are grouped together. Groups include forwards, defensemen, and goaltenders. The owner doesn’t have to create a team. They simply choose a player from each box. The first box may contain all elite forwards. These players include Connor McDavid, Leon Draisaitl, Nathan MacKinnon, and David Pastrnak. Owners select one of them. The league decides on the points system. The points are added up. Whoever has the most points at the season’s end wins.

ROTISSERIE LEAGUES

Rotisserie leagues hold a draft. Owners check their lineups every day. They move players around. If a player is scoring well, the owner wants him in the lineup.

Many leagues allow owners to change their lineups if a bench player starts scoring more consistently.

Owners want to be the best in as many categories as possible in rotisserie leagues.

Owners remove players who are not playing well. The person with the most points at the end of the season wins. The number of teams and stat categories determines the points awarded. Each stat category has points from one to the total number of players. For example, if a league had ten owners, each stat category could award up to ten points. Some examples of statistics include goals, assists, and shutouts. If an owner finishes first in a category, they would earn ten points. Second place would earn nine points. Third would be worth eight points. Last place earns one point. This is done for all the categories. Then the points are added up. The player with the highest total wins.

KEEPER LEAGUES

Keeper leagues are another way to play. They might be the closest thing to managing a real team. Keeper leagues begin with a draft. Owners draft a full team. At the end of the season, owners keep a set number of players. Other players are not kept. They are free to be drafted by someone else. Another draft is held at the beginning of the next season. Owners fill the spots on their teams. One or more trade days can be planned throughout the year depending on the league's rules.

Owners in a keeper league commit to the league for several seasons.

These leagues let their teams trade future draft picks, just like the NHL.

Waiver days happen throughout the season. These days are important.

They help owners improve their lineups. Owners can change their teams. This can be because of injuries. An NHLer who can't play won't earn points. The owner needs to replace him. The player then goes on the waivers page. This frees up a roster spot. Owners add an active player to replace the injured one. The dropped player can be picked up by another owner. However, they must have room for him. An owner may also waive a player because of poor play. Finding the right replacement takes some thought. "When in doubt, look to ice time," says Rick Seto of Bleacher Report. "As much hockey as we think we know, we don't know more than an NHL head coach. If a coach is giving more ice time to someone, that player must be doing something right."[5]

Many keeper leagues track the NHL salary cap. This requires strategy to build a team. Owners must stay under the cap. Stars like Erik Karlsson have a high salary.

ICE TIME

The NHL's website has ice time information. The NHL puts out a sheet with breakdowns for each player. They post statistics after every game. A player's NHL biography also provides a list of ice times at a glance.

If a league uses the salary cap to build teams, owners need to be mindful of how much players cost.

Owners must pick less expensive players for other positions. This gets harder as the team fills up. Like other leagues, different stats are tracked. The most popular are goals, assists, and goaltender wins.

Points are added up at the end of the season. Whoever has the highest score is the winner.

HEAD-TO-HEAD LEAGUES

Head-to-head leagues have two teams that play against each other. Owners earn points in different categories. They can include points, assists, and goaltender wins.

SALARY CAP

The NHL salary cap has two parts. It has a low and a high number. The low number is the smallest amount a team can pay its players. Teams must spend at least this amount. The high number is the most a team can spend. They cannot spend more.

People who want one-on-one competition can join a head-to-head league.

Other categories include power play goals, hits, and shots on goal. The matchup lasts for a set period of time. A week is common.

Each team adds up their totals. The owner with the most points wins. League standings are decided by each team's win, loss, and tie record. Head-to-head leagues often have playoffs. The top four teams face off. The top team plays the fourth-place team. The second- and third-place teams play each other. The winners from those matchups battle to decide the champion.

Owners can join any type of league. But it is important to do research. Studying players makes things easier. Owners are prepared for the draft. "When researching players before the draft, make lists to keep yourself organized," said Beneteau. "It's one thing to read up on a bunch of fantasy players to watch, but it's even better if you bring pre-planned notes to the draft. There is no point putting stars like Connor McDavid or Patrick Kane on these lists, as they are obvious picks. Instead, focus on players who could provide value in later rounds, and players who you want to avoid at all costs."[6]

Owners should plan for late in the draft when there are no stars left.

CHAPTER THREE

HOW DO OWNERS DRAFT TEAMS?

There are different ways to draft a team. Some leagues simply have owners make a list of players. Other owners have more to think about. They need more strategy. Drafts keep participants from choosing the same players. Every league is different when it comes to drafting. Some

There are many different types of drafts. A league can choose whichever style works best for them.

allow many players. Some leagues only let owners have a handful of players. A league might allow ten forwards, six defensemen, two goaltenders, and four bench spots.

Drafting a team can take several hours. Some leagues like to do it in person and throw a party to make it more fun.

STANDARD LINEAR DRAFT

In standard drafts, a team is given the same position in each round. A team could be given fourth position. They would always pick fourth. The position may be decided at random. It can also be decided by the finishing position of each team from the last season. Each team picks one player every round. This repeats until every team is full. Teams always pick in the same order. This can make things unfair. If one team is always last, they will not have the same talent as the team picking first.

SNAKE DRAFT

The snake draft is one of the most common draft styles. It is simple. It gives all teams a chance to draft some talent. Teams are given a draft position. This is done like a standard draft. Some leagues decide the order randomly. Others use the finishing positions of the last season. In the first round, the teams select their picks in order. But in the second round, the order is reversed. The team that picked last now selects first. The order goes back to top to bottom for the third round. Then it reverses for the fourth round. It continues in this pattern. The rounds finish when every team has a full lineup.

Both snake and standard drafts can be set up online. Some websites will help with drafting. The owner gives the website a list of players. The site will then select the best

Linear and Snake Drafts

Linear Draft

	Team Order									
Round 1	1	2	3	4	5	6	7	8	9	10
Round 2	1	2	3	4	5	6	7	8	9	10
Round 3	1	2	3	4	5	6	7	8	9	10

Snake Draft

	Team Order									
Round 1	1	2	3	4	5	6	7	8	9	10
Round 2	10	9	8	7	6	5	4	3	2	1
Round 3	1	2	3	4	5	6	7	8	9	10

Linear and snake drafts are similar. They both assign owners a position. Owners pick a player when it is their turn. Linear drafts use the same order. Snake drafts reverse after every round. Both styles repeat until every team is full.

available player each round. This can be a good choice for first-time fantasy players. The site does all the work.

NHL stars like Alex Ovechkin cost a lot in auctions. Fantasy teams can rarely afford to buy more than one or two star players.

AUCTIONS

Auctions are a fun way to add more strategy. Leagues set an imaginary budget. The NHL's salary cap is an easy choice. Participants then bid on different players.

The person who bids the most gets the player. Star players are always popular. Owners must spend more to get them on their teams. Participants need to carefully spend their fantasy budgets. They must try to land sleepers for a low amount.

STRATEGY PREPARATION FOR DRAFT DAY

"When preparing for your draft, you will likely confront several dilemmas," says Matt Cubeta of NHL.com. "What position do you draft in the first round? When do you grab your first goalie? How about your first defenseman? Before answering these questions, you need to pick a strategy and stick to it."[7]

One strategy is to draft a balanced team in all positions. Select the best available players in early rounds. Cover each position: forward, defense, and goaltenders. Then the owner can look over their team. They can fill out the rest of their roster during later rounds. An owner considers the statistics used by their league. They want players that score the most points. Maybe a league awards points for faceoff wins. The owner can then add a player who may not score many goals but wins a lot of faceoffs.

Owners must make a plan and identify their top choices ahead of time to be prepared for a draft.

Another strategy is to focus on one position. This is often forwards or goaltenders. Drafting high-scoring forwards leads to a lot of points. Owners want a steady goaltender. They don't need the best. Teams want a goaltender with more wins than losses. Selecting two great goaltenders early can pay off. The best goaltenders are harder to get. There are fewer goaltenders than forwards. Also, an injured goaltender will be harder to replace. Top goaltenders like Jordan Binnington and Marc-Andre Fleury are usually drafted early.

STATISTICS TO WATCH

Nearly every league has the same basic stats. These are goals, assists, and goaltender wins. Star forwards will score lots of points. Do not forget about offensive defensemen. They make long passes.

A strong goaltender is necessary for any team.

They skate deep into the offensive zone. They pick up many assists. Owners should think about other statistics, too. This helps them draft the best team. A league may track fights. It might be smart to draft an enforcer.

Goaltenders often earn points in four categories. These are wins, goals-against average, save percentage, and shutouts. Goal-against average is the number of goals the goaltender allowed divided by the number of minutes he played. The lower the number, the fewer goals he allowed. The best goaltenders have low numbers. The save percentage shows the number of goals stopped by the goaltender. It is the number of saves divided by the amount of shots against him. In this case, a higher number is best.

Blocked shots are another popular statistic. Forwards can block shots. But this is often done by defensemen. They are closer to the net. They help the goaltender. "Stay-at-home" defensemen are less offense-minded. They often block many shots. They remain close to the goaltender.

BLUELINE BASICS

An example of an offensive defenseman is Erik Karlsson. An example of a defensive, or "stay at home," defenseman is Marc-Edouard Vlasic. An offensive defenseman will help more with points. But, if a goaltender isn't performing well, having a defensive-minded defenseman might help block more shots.

A league may also give points for shots on goal. These happen when a player shoots the puck toward the net but the goaltender stops it.

Some leagues record hits. Enforcers may be good for hit totals. However, they usually only play a few minutes each night. Many

DOUBLING UP ON POINTS TOTALS

Alex Ovechkin is a player who will score many points. He will also hit a lot of opposing players. But he is a popular player to draft. Dustin Byfuglien is a midlevel player. He is good for earning points and hits. He is more likely be available later in a draft. Milan Lucic is a defenseman who earns points for both blocked shots and hits.

don't score a lot. Scraps may only happen every few games. There are benefits to drafting an offensive player who likes to hit. Owners will gain points for both goals and hits.

Owners should take a closer look at their league's categories before the draft. It will help them predict which players will gain the highest totals.

CHAPTER FOUR

HOW DO OWNERS BUILD A WINNING TEAM?

Good research helps build a winning team. Owners want to be prepared. There are many resources to help. Hockey magazines are a good starting place. These come out before the season starts. Many include breakdowns of every NHL player. These breakdowns suggest

There are many resources online to help owners prepare for the season.

who to consider drafting. Magazines also include who to avoid.

Current information can be found online. The NHL's website keeps statistics. Fantasy hockey is more popular than ever. The NHL

It is best to keep a league's stat categories in mind when comparing different players.

has up-to-date stats for owners to use. This is helpful when an owner needs to add a player in the middle of a season. Owners can also stay updated on injuries. They can keep track of NHL trades.

DIG DEEPER

The amount of information owners need depends on their league. "Every fantasy league is different," says Steve Laidlaw of Sportsnet. "With every rule change comes an [adjustment] in player value. Factors like scoring system, number of teams, number of players you start, whether you start them weekly or nightly, etc., all influence what you should be looking for at the draft table."[8] Box leagues are easier. They focus on a few categories.

Box leagues focus on certain key categories, such as goaltender wins.

These may include goals, assists, and goaltender wins. Owners pick high-scoring forwards, offensive defensemen, and good goaltenders. "When in doubt, keep it simple: Take good players on good teams," says Myles Dichter of CBC Sports.[9]

Keeper, head-to-head, and rotisserie leagues need more research. Find a player's **average draft position (ADP)** from

WHERE DO ADP NUMBERS COME FROM?

Average Draft Position (ADP) comes from online leagues. Some sites have leagues with millions of people playing. ESPN and CBSSports are two examples. ADP is a number that these sites calculate. It is based on the number of owners drafting a certain player. It also depends on where in the draft that player is being taken. A player's ADP will rise or fall depending on their play during that NHL season. Nazem Kadri had a Yahoo! ADP of 150.8 before the 2012–13 season. He went on to score forty-four points. It was the most he had scored in his career. That meant for the next season, his ADP rose. Compare ADP numbers to a player's points totals for that year. This gives owners a better idea of where the player might be available.

Owners must consider many factors before adding a player to their team.

past seasons. Try a **mock draft** before the real thing. The best players are typically taken first. These picks will be obvious. Forwards like Connor McDavid and

Nathan MacKinnon will go quickly. Owners guess who might be available during their turn. They make a list of players. The list can help them be ready if their first choice is taken. They have another player ready to choose.

Dig deep into player information. One might score a lot of points. But he might get injured a lot. Sidney Crosby is one example. An injured player cannot be in the lineup. He will not pick up fantasy points. The owner will need to add another player. If a skater doesn't score enough points, the owner might go down in the standings.

Pay attention to on-ice time. More ice time means more chances to score. After goaltenders, defensemen play the most during games. Fourth-line forwards play the least. This doesn't mean they are a poor draft choice. Remember the

WATCH THOSE YOUNG GUNS

Keep an eye out for stories covering the American Hockey League (AHL). The AHL is where most signed young players spend their first NHL season. If an AHL player is doing well, he may be called up to play on an NHL team. Goaltender Mackenzie Blackwood is one example. Players who come from the AHL are available to scoop up on waivers.

It is a good idea to draft a tough player in a league that counts hits or penalty minutes.

categories for points in any league. Is there a category for penalty minutes? NHL coaches often put their tougher players on the fourth line. These are players who might get into fights. They usually play rough.

Players can surprise owners. Some may play better or worse than expected. Good owners adjust their teams as needed.

They have a lot of penalties. In this case, it might be good to draft a fourth-line player. They will not be on the ice for very long. But they will likely get points when they are out looking for opponents to smash.

READ THE REPORTS

Technology makes it easy for an owner to find reports about anything. They can look at a rookie's junior hockey numbers. This gives an idea of how he might play in the NHL.

Reading news from sports reporters is useful. Reporters spend a lot of time with NHL teams. If a reporter sees a player having problems with the coach, they may write about it. These tidbits are important. A player arguing with a coach may be punished. He could be benched for a game. If he's not playing, he cannot

Owners want to predict sleepers who will be easy to draft and still earn many points.

score points. Sports reporters also give other information. They report a game's lineup. If a third-line player is moved to the second line, that means more on-ice time. It also means a better chance to gain points. Reporters share which goaltenders are starting. Owners can decide which one they would like to put in that night.

Do not forget about sleepers. Once again, websites can be the best source for knowledge. Look for feature stories on players. Maybe they were traded in the offseason. They could be expected to play well with their new teammates. What if a young player did not play a lot last season? Did he still score points? That could mean more ice time this season. The more an owner knows about NHLers, the better.

Fantasy hockey is a great game for any NHL fan. Owners get to experience hockey in a new way. They can compete with their friends. They can learn more about their favorite players and teams, all without leaving their couch. Win or lose, they will have fun and find more reasons to cheer about the greatest sport on ice.

The hard work of managing a team pays off when the team does well.

GLOSSARY

average draft position (ADP)

The position where a player is most often drafted on fantasy websites.

draft manager

The person who sets up and runs the draft.

empty-net goal

A goal scored after the goalie has been pulled in the final minutes of the game.

healthy scratches

NHL players who sit out one game or more for multiple reasons, such as low goal scoring or being an extra player on an already full roster.

mock draft

Practice drafts used as a tool to help owners prepare for their real draft.

sleepers

Players who at first are not expected to perform well but end up scoring many points.

waiver

When owners release players from their team and another owner can then choose to add that player to their roster.

SOURCE NOTES

CHAPTER ONE: WHAT IS FANTASY HOCKEY?

1. Matt Larkin, "Top 10 Fantasy Hockey Sleeper Picks for 2019-20," *The Hockey News*, September 19, 2019. www.thehockeynews.com.

2. Quoted in Tal Pinchevsky, "Fantasy Hockey Has Roots with Neil Smith, MSG," *NHL.com*, September 2, 2011. www.nhl.com.

3. Quoted in Pinchevsky, "Fantasy Hockey Has Roots with Neil Smith, MSG."

CHAPTER TWO: WHICH LEAGUE TO CHOOSE?

4. Josh Beneteau, "Fantasy Hockey Draft Kit 2019: Five Key Draft-Night Strategies," *Sportsnet*, September 20, 2019. www.sportsnet.ca.

5. Rick Seto, "Fantasy Hockey Advice: Draft with These Strategies in Mind," *Bleacher Report*, September 26, 2011. www.bleacherreport.com.

6. Beneteau, "Fantasy Hockey Draft Kit 2019: Five Key Draft-Night Strategies."

CHAPTER THREE: HOW DO OWNERS DRAFT TEAMS?

7. Matt Cubeta, "The ABC's of Fantasy Hockey," *NHL.com*, August 22, 2011. www.nhl.com.

CHAPTER FOUR: HOW DO OWNERS BUILD A WINNING TEAM?

8. Steve Laidlaw, "How to Execute the Perfect Fantasy Hockey Draft," *Sportsnet*, September 26, 2017. www.sports.ca.

9. Myles Dichter, "How to Outsmart Your Friends and Win Your Fantasy Hockey League," *CBC Sports*, October 2, 2018. www.cbc.ca/sports.

FOR FURTHER RESEARCH

BOOKS

Shane Frederick, *Fantasy Hockey Math: Using STATS to Score Big in Your League*. North Mankato, MN: Capstone Press, 2017.

National Hockey League, *National Hockey League Official Guide & Record Book 2019*. Chicago, IL: Triumph Books, 2018.

Mike Ryan, *Hockey Now!: The Biggest Stars of the NHL*. Richmond Hill, ON: Firefly Books, 2019.

INTERNET SOURCES

Matt Cubeta, "The ABC's of Fantasy Hockey," *NHL*, August 22, 2012. www.nhl.com.

Pete Jensen, "NHL.com Fantasy Hockey Glossary," *NHL*, September 23, 2016. www.nhl.com.

Steve Laidlaw, "How to Execute the Perfect Fantasy Hockey Draft," *Sportsnet*, September 26, 2017. www.sportsnet.ca.

WEBSITES

Dobber Hockey

www.dobberhockey.com

Dobber Hockey features fantasy hockey information, starting player information, rankings, and tools for building and maintaining a fantasy hockey team.

NHL.com

www.nhl.com

NHL.com is the National Hockey League's official website and includes hockey news and player statistics.

Yahoo! Fantasy

hockey.fantasysports.yahoo.com

Yahoo has a popular fantasy football league hosting service as well as breaking news and analysis from around the NHL.

INDEX

American Hockey League (AHL), 66
auction, 4, 48–49
average draft position (ADP), 63

Beneteau, Josh, 25–27, 39–40
Blackwood, Mackenzie, 66
box league, 4, 24, 27–28, 61
Brodeur, Martin, 21
Burns, Brent, 8–10
Byfuglien, Dustin, 56

Crosby, Sidney, 65
Cubeta, Matt, 49

defenseman, 5, 27, 43, 49, 50, 53, 55, 56, 62, 65–66
Dichter, Myles, 62
draft, 4, 15, 17, 19–20, 21, 28, 32–33, 39–40, 42–47, 49–53, 56, 57, 58, 63, 67
draft manager, 27

enforcer, 53, 56

forward, 5, 27–28, 43, 50–52, 55, 62, 64, 66

goaltender, 19, 22, 27, 36–37, 43, 50–52, 54–56, 61–62, 65–66, 71
Gretzky, Wayne, 21

head-to-head league, 4, 37-39, 62

ice time, 34–35, 65, 71

Kane, Patrick, 40
Karlsson, Eric, 35, 55
keeper league, 4, 23, 25, 32, 35, 62

Laidlaw, Steve, 61
Larkin, Matt, 16

MacKinnon, Nathan, 28, 64
McDavid, Conner, 28, 40, 64
mock draft, 63

Off-Ice Hockey League (OIHL), 18–20
Ovechkin, Alex, 56

Rosen, Sam, 19–20
rotisserie league, 4, 23, 28–31, 62

salary cap, 35, 37, 48
Seto, Rick, 34
simulated hockey, 21
sleepers, 16, 49, 71
Smith, Neil, 17–18

trades, 15, 25, 32–33, 61, 71

waivers, 33–34, 66

IMAGE CREDITS

Cover: © Andy Martin Jr/Alamy
5: © Tom Wang/Shutterstock Images
7: © Antonio Guillem/Shutterstock Images
8: © Kaytoo/Shutterstock Images
11: © Adwo/Shutterstock Images
12: © Scott Prokop/Shutterstock Images
15: © Photo Works/Shutterstock Images
17: © Pabkov/Shutterstock Images
20: © Kostas Lymperopoulos/Cal Sport Media/AP Images
22: © Syda Productions/Shutterstock Images
25: © Prostock-studio/Shutterstock Images
26: © Jai Agnish/Shutterstock Images
29: © Kyle Besler/Shutterstock Images
30: © Kyle Besler/Shutterstock Images
33: © Shift Drive/Shutterstock Images
36: © Ross D. Franklin/AP Images
38: © Prostock-studio/Shutterstock Images
41: © Photo Works/Shutterstock Images
43: © Konstantin Chagin/Shutterstock Images
44: © Monkey Business Images/Shutterstock Images
47: © Red Line Editorial
48: © Nick Wass/AP Images
51: © Jai Agnish/Shutterstock Images
53: © Ryan Morgan/Shutterstock Images
59: © AlenD/Shutterstock Images
60: © Jai Agnish/Shutterstock Images
62: © Jai Agnish/Shutterstock Images
64: © Jai Agnish/Shutterstock Images
67: © Jai Agnish/Shutterstock Images
68: © Kyle Besler/Shutterstock Images
70: © Jai Agnish/Shutterstock Images
73: © Antlio/Shutterstock Images

ABOUT THE AUTHOR

Erin Nicks is originally from Thunder Bay, Ontario. She has written about hockey for the past twenty years. Her work has been featured in newspapers and websites, including Yahoo! and NHL.com. Her favorite NHL players of all time are Daniel Alfredsson, Bryan Smolinski, and Dominik Hasek. She currently lives in Ottawa, Ontario.